0°

30°

Queen Maud Land

ar Plateau

th Pole

80°

Transantarctic Mountains

ss Ice Shelf

Greetings from
Antarctica

The South Pole
Wednesday 19 December

Dear Daniel,

Here is the letter which I promised
to write to you from the South Pole.

Imagine how excited I am to be here
at last, following in the footsteps of
so many famous explorers. I will
send you more soon.

Love, Sara

PETER BEDRICK BOOKS
NEW YORK

To dear Daniel, of course

Published by
Peter Bedrick Books
156 Fifth Avenue
New York, NY 10010

Commissioning editor: Hazel Songhurst
Designers: The Design Works, Reading
Editor: Hazel Songhurst
Illustrations: Peter Bull Art Studio

Picture acknowledgements:
Bryan & Cherry Alexander: cover (l), 5(l), 21(bc),
22(br), 23(l and cr), 24(ct), 25(b), 31(tl), 32(br),
34(l), 38, 41(cr), all by Ann Hawthorne, 5(r), 7,
26(br), 27(cl), 39, all by Hans Reinhard, 20(bl),
28(tr), 29(tr), 33(c and br), all Paul Drummond,
34 (b) NASA. Popperfoto: 13 (tl and bl),
37 (tl, tc and tr)

All other photographs by Sara Wheeler

Wheeler, Sara.
    Greetings from Antarctica / [text and
photographs, Sara Wheeler]. -- 1st American ed.
    p. cm.
    Includes index.
    Summary: The author tells the story of her
experiences living and working in Antarctica.
Includes letters and photographs to her godson.
    ISBN 0-87226-295-2 (hardcover)
    1. Wheeler, Sara--Correspondence--Juvenile
literature.
2. Antarctica--Description and travel--Juvenile
literature.
3. Travelers--Great Britain--Biography--Juvenile
literature.
[1. Wheeler, Sara. 2. Antarctica. 3. Letters.]
I. Title.
G875.W44A3 1999
919.8'9'04--DC21   98-37203
                                        CIP
                                        AC

Printed and bound in Portugal
by Edições ASA

First American Edition 1999

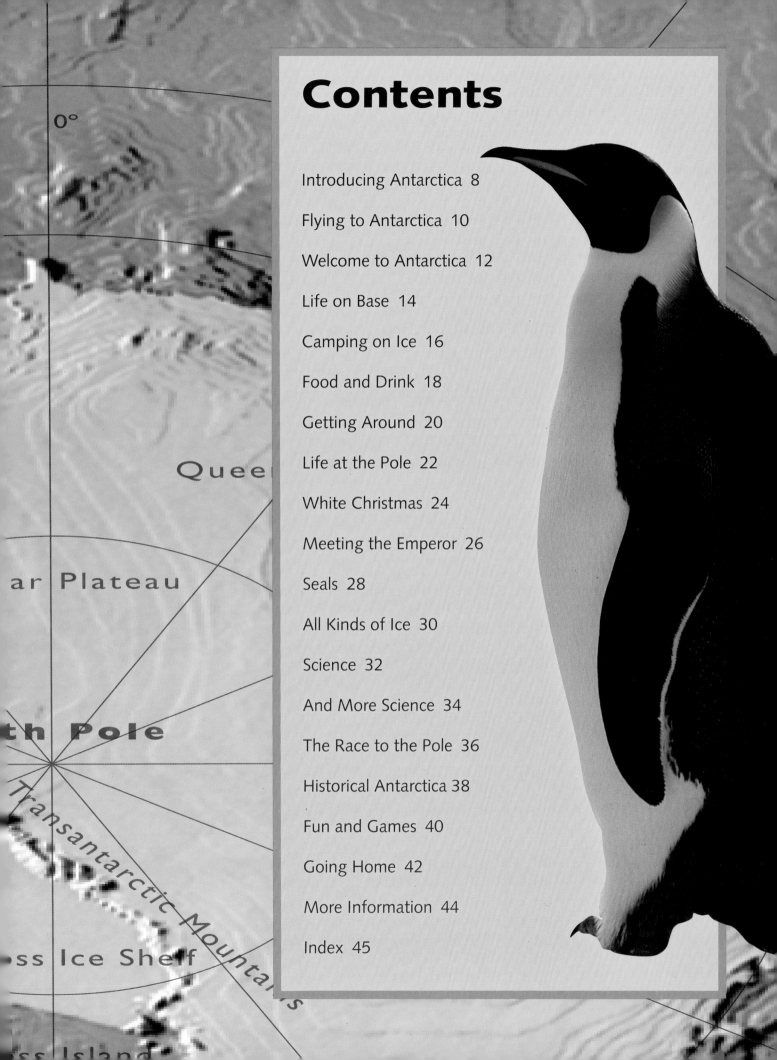

Contents

Introducing Antarctica 8

Flying to Antarctica 10

Welcome to Antarctica 12

Life on Base 14

Camping on Ice 16

Food and Drink 18

Getting Around 20

Life at the Pole 22

White Christmas 24

Meeting the Emperor 26

Seals 28

All Kinds of Ice 30

Science 32

And More Science 34

The Race to the Pole 36

Historical Antarctica 38

Fun and Games 40

Going Home 42

More Information 44

Index 45

Introducing Antarctica

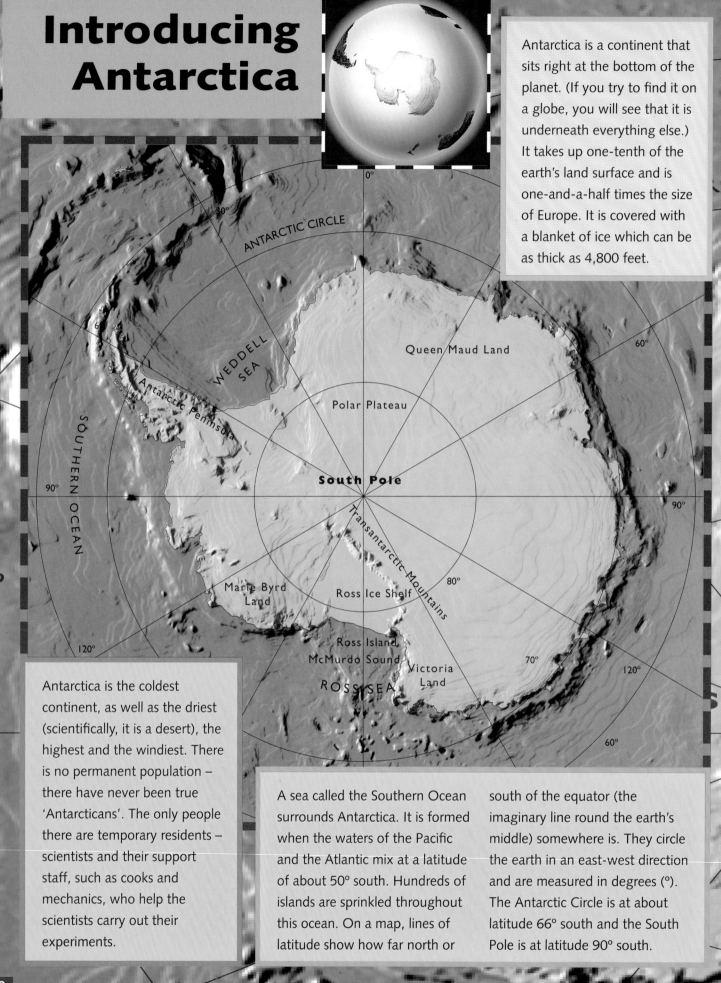

Antarctica is a continent that sits right at the bottom of the planet. (If you try to find it on a globe, you will see that it is underneath everything else.) It takes up one-tenth of the earth's land surface and is one-and-a-half times the size of Europe. It is covered with a blanket of ice which can be as thick as 4,800 feet.

0°

30°

ANTARCTIC CIRCLE

60°

Queen Maud Land

60°

WEDDELL SEA

Antarctic Peninsula

Polar Plateau

SOUTHERN OCEAN

South Pole

90°

90°

Transantarctic Mountains

80°

Marie Byrd Land

Ross Ice Shelf

70°

120°

Ross Island

McMurdo Sound

Victoria Land

120°

ROSS SEA

60°

Antarctica is the coldest continent, as well as the driest (scientifically, it is a desert), the highest and the windiest. There is no permanent population – there have never been true 'Antarcticans'. The only people there are temporary residents – scientists and their support staff, such as cooks and mechanics, who help the scientists carry out their experiments.

A sea called the Southern Ocean surrounds Antarctica. It is formed when the waters of the Pacific and the Atlantic mix at a latitude of about 50° south. Hundreds of islands are sprinkled throughout this ocean. On a map, lines of latitude show how far north or south of the equator (the imaginary line round the earth's middle) somewhere is. They circle the earth in an east-west direction and are measured in degrees (°). The Antarctic Circle is at about latitude 66° south and the South Pole is at latitude 90° south.

How cold is it in Antarctica?

Colder than you can possibly imagine! During the summer, which means from October to March, temperatures can climb to several degrees Celsius above freezing. But in the winter, which is from April to September, it falls much lower – even to -128°F. When it is that cold, a mug of boiling water thrown in the air would freeze before it hit the ice. The mean (average) annual temperature on the continent is 0°F.

Here is a graph to show you just how cold it gets. The temperature varies according to where you are on the continent. It is warmer on the coast, and gets colder as you approach the middle. At the South Pole, the mean temperature in January, which is the height of summer, is -28°C. Sometimes scientists have to use fridges to keep their samples warm.

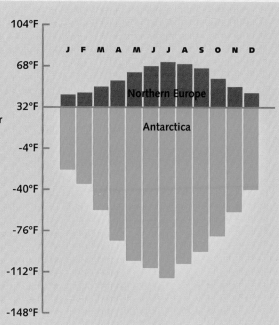

J F M A M J J A S O N D

104°F

68°F

Northern Europe

32°F

Antarctica

-4°F

-40°F

-76°F

-112°F

-148°F

This is me standing in front of the Barne glacier. The Barne is a huge block of ice locked into the frozen sea.

Endless nights and days

Summer in Antarctica means six months of continuous daylight. From October to March, the region inside the Antarctic circle continuously faces the sun's light. In winter, the opposite happens and Antarctica is tilted away from the sun, plunging it into six months of endless darkness.

International cooperation

Although seven countries claim a slice of Antarctica, the Antarctic Treaty doesn't recognize any territorial claims. It says that Antarctica is for everybody. It is the only place on earth which nobody owns. I have noticed that all different nationalities help each other down here. I wish it could be like that back at home.

This diagram shows the 7 territorial claims on Antarctica. You can see how some overlap.

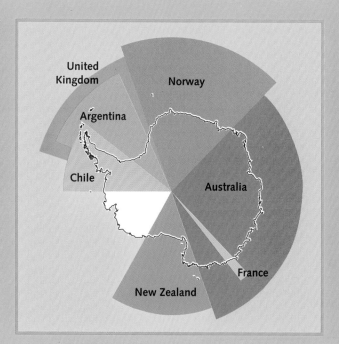

United Kingdom

Norway

Argentina

Chile

Australia

New Zealand

France

Flying to Antarctica

I am here

This is the Hercules plane which flew me to Antarctica.

Ross Ice Shelf
Friday 2 December

Dear Daniel,

I flew down here from Christchurch, New Zealand in a Hercules plane belonging to the American Navy. Because it is a military plane it has no windows and I had to be strapped into a red webbing seat! There was no heating either, so I had to wear all my special Antarctic clothes, and no soundproofing, so I put in earplugs. The journey took eight hours, then the plane landed on skis on the Ross Ice Shelf.

When the plane door opened it was like stepping into a deep freeze.

More soon.

Love from Sara

This photo shows how the ice covering Antarctica forms glaciers when it meets the sea. Most of the sea here is frozen.

Volcanoes

Antarctica has at least two active volcanoes. The photo shows Mount Erebus on Ross Island. It was named by the English explorer James Clark Ross after the ship in which he sailed south between 1839 and 1843. He was the first sailor to cross the Antarctic Circle. Erebus is 12,138 feet tall, and you can usually see puffs of smoke coming out of the top.

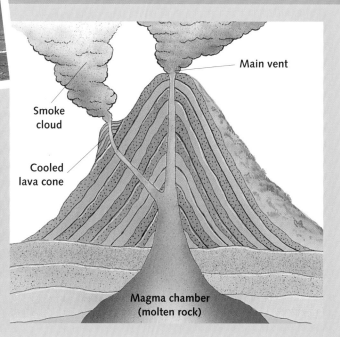

This drawing shows a slice through a volcano. It is actually a mountain made from molten rock (lava) that has risen up from deep underground. When gases collect near the surface explosions happen, shooting out burning lava and clouds of smoke.

Main vent

Smoke cloud

Cooled lava cone

Magma chamber (molten rock)

Transport on ice

If you have ever tried walking on a frozen path you'll know that ice is very slippery underfoot. That's why people wear skis on snow – to give them more surface area to stand on. Well, planes need skis if they are going to land on ice otherwise they skid around all over the place. Their skis are made of metal and they are much bigger and heavier than the ones people wear. They can be taken off when the plane arrives back on dry land.

This Twin Otter plane is fitted with skis.

Land vehicles are used in Antarctica, but they have to be specially adapted with caterpillar tracks so they have a greater area of contact with the ice and don't slide around. The tracks move much more slowly than wheels – but they are safer.

This is me perching on the caterpillar track of a small truck. My skis are sticking up at the back.

Welcome to Antarctica

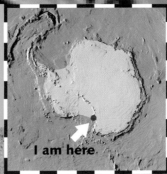

I am here.

In this picture I am wearing my identification tags as earrings.

Ross Ice Shelf
Sunday 4 December

Dear Daniel

You can't imagine how long it takes to get dressed here. Each morning I put on two sets of long-sleeved thermal underwear, including long johns; a thick wool shirt; a pair of salopettes, which are special dungarees designed for snow and ice; a fleece cardigan-type jacket and a huge parka. On my feet I have two pairs of socks, bootliners (these are a bit like the bootees babies wear) and boots, on my hands a pair of glove liners and two pairs of gloves, and on my head a balaclava and thermal hat. It takes hours! We also have to wear metal identification tags all the time. Most people hang them round their necks - but I have found another way (see the small photograph above).

More soon.

Love from Sara

Turning on your ice boots

I have a pair of rubberised white ice boots which have a layer of air trapped between two layers of rubber. This air acts as insulation. The only trouble is, you have to remember to change the pressure of the air when you travel in certain types of planes – otherwise the boots may explode! To do this there is a valve on the side which must be turned on and off.

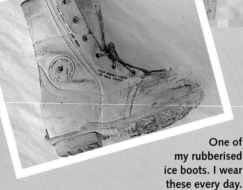

One of my rubberised ice boots. I wear these every day.

Early explorers

In the early days of polar exploration men wore furs like the Inuit people who live in Arctic regions. The clothes were very warm – but if the fur got wet it was very heavy too, and when it froze it was like being in a suit of armor. Sometimes the men had to use tin openers to get their clothes off! Today's high-tech fabrics dry very quickly.

In the early 1900s, explorers like Roald Amundsen wore full fur protection.

Captain Evans of Scott's Antarctic expedition in 1911.

Insulating layers

All those layers of clothes I wrote about in my letter trap air between them. The air acts as insulation – which means that three thin layers of fabric keep me much warmer than one thick layer. The system means that I can take off layers of clothing if I get overheated while working on the ice. Believe it or not, you can get hot and sweaty, even here.

This is me out on the ice, wearing a parka with my name on it.

Several layers of clothes trap body heat to insulate us from the cold.

- Body
- Warm air
- Clothes
- Cold air

In an Antarctic camp finding a warm place to rest is really important. Here is my friend Lucia having a snooze in a wooden crate.

Goggles and glacier glasses protect our eyes from the glare of the sun reflecting off the snow. Snow-blindness is pretty scary. The bright light stops your eyes from working properly for a while and you can only see white light.

This is my friend Steffen, an American geologist. He's all dressed up in his hooded parka, special cold-weather hat with ear-flaps and also a pair of glacier glasses.

Life on Base

I am here

Antarctic stations

Stations, or bases, are dotted all over Antarctica. Most of them are near the coast. There are approximately two hundred in total, but some are little more than a handful of huts. Each base is owned by a particular nation, and most are only open during the summer months. The Americans have the largest Antarctic program. Their three bases are called McMurdo, Palmer and Amundsen-Scott South Pole Station.

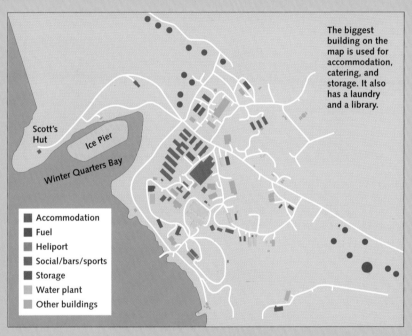

Scott's Hut

Ice Pier

Winter Quarters Bay

The biggest building on the map is used for accommodation, catering, and storage. It also has a laundry and a library.

- ■ Accommodation
- ■ Fuel
- ■ Heliport
- ■ Social/bars/sports
- ■ Storage
- ■ Water plant
- ■ Other buildings

This map shows McMurdo Base, where I had my first taste of life in the Antarctic. It is the largest settlement on the continent.

Keeping healthy

Antarctica is a healthy place because it's too cold for germs, though the low temperatures sometimes make fillings fall out of our teeth. We have to make sure we keep warm and notice signs of frostbite, such as stinging fingers.

New Zealanders in the kitchen of their base on Ross Island.

New Zealand claims a large slice of Antarctica. Its base, called Scott Base, is very near McMurdo on Ross Island.

Making water

On base we get water by a process known as reverse osmosis. This is when all the salt is forced out of seawater. The seawater is stored on one side of a membrane (a thin skin) before being pumped through it to the other side.

The membrane acts as a filter, removing the salt from the seawater and leaving pure, salt free water behind.

Drinking 'seawater' tea outside the main building at Rothera, the British base on the Antarctic Peninsula.

SOUTHERN OCEAN

McMurdo
Tuesday 6 December

McMurdo Station on Ross Island – the largest base in Antarctica.

Dear Daniel,

I am staying at McMurdo, the main American base in Antarctica. A base is where scientists prepare to go into remote camps to do their experiments. They get their equipment ready here – it is like a staging post. A lot of people work on the base to help the scientists – some are engineers and others are mechanics or cooks. We live either in dormitories or in small rooms, and we sleep on bunk beds. Nothing grows in Antarctica so all the food has to be flown in. But I met some people who are growing vegetables just in water, without any soil.

Please write back soon!

Love from Sara

Hydroponics

Hydroponics is a way of growing plants without soil. The roots of hydroponically grown plants live in water all the time – but you have to add special nutrients to the water so the plants have food.

At McMurdo people enjoy eating hydroponically grown vegetables they have picked themselves.

ss Ice Shelf

Camping on Ice

I am here

Mackay Glacier
Saturday 10 December

Dear Daniel,

This week I am visiting a group of scientists near the Mackay Glacier. They are drilling holes in the frozen sea and sending a remote operated vehicle down to the bottom. The vehicle transmits pictures of the seabed that we watch on a screen in a small tent. I have just been watching sea anemones swaying in the current.

I have put my tent up on the ice here. I have to put a board underneath my sleeping bag, otherwise the heat from my body makes the ice melt and I get soggy.

Love from Sara

I took this photograph while lying in my sleeping bag looking out of the tent flaps.

An Antarctic toilet. The box sits over a hole drilled in the ice lid of the frozen sea. Beware of seals popping up!

Looking under the ice

The scientists are trying to see what the seabed looks like under its ice lid. They are particularly interested in the bottom of glaciers – what they call the grounding line. Remote operated vehicles are sent under the ice with cameras attached to them to send back pictures to the surface.

Steve sends the remote operated vehicle down under the ice.

Building an igloo

Igloos are dome-shaped houses made of ice blocks. I had to learn to build one as part of my survival training, in case I ever need shelter in an emergency. Here you can see me and some scientist friends building one for fun. The Inuit people from the Arctic used to live in igloos, but not many do now. In some areas of Canada children still take igloo-building lessons at school.

We cut blocks out of the ice sheet with special ice saws.

Then we lay them in a circle.

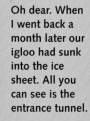

We piled the blocks up in a spiral shape with the top ones leaning in to make a dome.

Bruno and Mark, a pair of American scientists, are using ice blocks to make an arch above the entrance hole.

Oh dear. When I went back a month later our igloo had sunk into the ice sheet. All you can see is the entrance tunnel.

Food and Drink

I am here

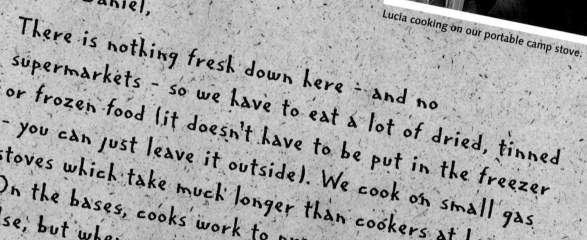

Lucia cooking on our portable camp stove.

Ice Stream B
Wednesday 14 December

Dear Daniel,

There is nothing fresh down here — and no supermarkets — so we have to eat a lot of dried, tinned or frozen food (it doesn't have to be put in the freezer — you can just leave it outside). We cook on small gas stoves which take much longer than cookers at home. On the bases, cooks work to prepare meals for everyone else, but when we are in field camps we take it in turns. Yesterday I made spaghetti with tomato paste and cheese out of a tin, followed by dehydrated strawberries which tasted like cardboard.

I miss apples and oranges — please send me some!

Love from Sara

Corn cakes made by Lucia.

Grub up!

Food and other supplies arrive at camp by plane or helicopter. Everyone helps to unload, because if the pilot switches off the engine in these temperatures he'll never get it started up again. At camp there is no reverse osmosis to change seawater into fresh water: we have to make all our own water from ice.

Here we are unloading a Twin Otter supply plane at camp. There was a letter from you on board, Daniel.

Use your imagination

When you can't go shopping you have to make do with what you have. Last week we mixed instant mashed potato powder with packet soup to make a kind of savoury porridge. Don't try it at home, Daniel!

Waiting for dinner.

Antarctic bread and butter pudding

Ingredients
Bread (usually very stale in Antarctica)
Sugar
Dried milk powder
Dried egg powder
Raisins
Cinnamon

Chop some ice off a glacier and melt it to make water. Use the water to make milk and egg with the powders. Soak slices of stale bread in the liquid. Layer the bread in a dish, sprinkling raisins, cinnamon and sugar between the layers.

You need a portable oven for this dish – some camps have them.

Cook the pudding for 45 minutes, then call everyone into the tent to eat. You'll have to imagine the custard.

Cooking for ten in a small tent

It's not easy! You have to prepare in advance too – sometimes by keeping tins in the warm tent all night so they thaw in time for breakfast.

Water, water everywhere...

And all of it frozen. Here I am fetching ice in a banana sledge to melt for water. Can you guess why it's called a banana?

This is the pick I use to break off chunks of ice to melt to make water.

Imagine – I have to go and hack out a chunk of ice with my pick every time I want to make a meal, or just a cup of tea!

19

Getting Around

I am here

Flying in Antarctica

Hercules and Twin Otter planes are the main forms of transport for covering the huge distances of Antarctica. Helicopters are used to travel shorter distances – usually up to about 186 miles. Sometimes helicopters fly with cargo dangling underneath on the ends of ropes. This is known as 'carrying an external load'.

Helicopters are used widely in the Antarctic. This one is about to pick up cargo from a science camp.

Inside a helicopter – my view from the back seat.

Supplies ready to be loaded into a Twin Otter plane.

Traveling by land and sea

Sometimes journeys are unsuitable for planes or helicopters. On the ice we use skidoos (sometimes called snow-mobiles), which are motorcycles fitted with skis instead of wheels. An inflatable boat with an outboard motor is used where the seawater isn't frozen.

These scientists are using a skidoo to pull a Nansen sledge – like a train engine pulling a carriage. Riding on the sledge is great fun.

Vasco steering an inflatable boat called a Zodiac.

Central West Antarctica
Sunday 18 December

Supplies ready to be loaded into a helicopter belonging to the Italian Antarctic program.

Dear Daniel,

I have been traveling to some more field camps. I love going by helicopter because you get such a great view. You have to speak to the pilot over headphones. It's important to remember to say 'Over' when you have finished speaking. We keep emergency gear in the back of the helicopter in case we have to make an unscheduled stop in bad weather.

When we are in camp we travel about on skidoos, which are motorcycles on skis. I think I've just about learned to ride one without falling off.

Over and out.

Sara

An Antarctic petrol station – barrels of fuel on the ice.

Nansen sledges

These wooden sledges were designed a century ago by a Norwegian called Fridjhof Nansen. They have hardly changed since then and are still widely used. They can be pulled by people or skidoos and are easy to repair.

Here is my Nansen sledge, partially loaded with my gear.

These geologists are using a Nansen sledge pulled by skidoos.

Life at the Pole

I am here

My bed in a dormitory hut at the South Pole.

The South Pole
Thursday 22 December
Temperature: -20°F

Dear Daniel,

I flew 746 miles from the Ross Ice Shelf to get here and when I did I had such a shock - the scientists and support workers had put up this sign of Elvis! There are a hundred people here at the moment, all American except me. Soon after the plane had landed I was given a camp bed in a long hut, but most people live under a great big dome specially designed to keep warm without burning too much fuel. Near the dome is the pole itself - at latitude 90° south.

Imagine - here I am right down at the bottom of the world!
Can you find the spot on a globe?

Love, Sara

GRACELAND →

Me at the signpost showing the distances to different cities around the world.

The South Pole

The marker at the Pole has to be moved each year, as over a 12-month period the ice slides about 32 feet over the land far below it. The scientists seen in the photograph below are preparing to reposition the marker.

American workers at the South Pole base gather under the Stars and Stripes. The signpost marks the Geographic South Pole.

When you stand at the South Pole, whichever direction you face is north. No other compass point exists.

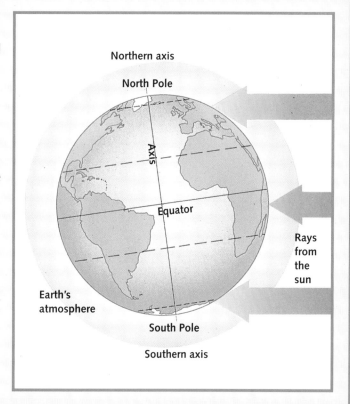

The flags of twelve nations fly at the Pole. The short ceremonial marker is in the center.

The bottom of the world

The earth spins around an imaginary line called its axis. If you look at the drawing you can see that the South Pole is at the southern axis of the earth's spin. The altitude here is 9,120 feet above sea level, which means that I am sitting on a layer of ice almost one third of the height of Mount Everest. Also, the earth's atmosphere is at its most shallow at the poles. The combination of high altitude and shallow atmosphere means that the human body receives only about half of its normal oxygen supply. I get out of breath if I walk back to my hut too quickly.

To reach the poles, the sun's rays have to travel further than they do to get to the equator, the imaginary line round the middle of the globe. That is why lands near the poles are colder than lands near the equator.

Northern axis

North Pole

Axis

Equator

Rays from the sun

Earth's atmosphere

South Pole

Southern axis

White Christmas

I am here

Perfect silence

The station at 90° south belongs to the American Antarctic Program, and they named it after two great polar explorers, Roald Amundsen and Robert Falcon Scott. It is located at probably the most remote place on earth and as you might expect, it is very, very quiet.

The geodesic dome at the Pole, looking from the meteorological tower. Most people here live under the dome.

Me on the ice plateau.

I borrowed some cross-country skis and took a short trip out on to the polar plateau. Away from the buildings of the base itself, when the wind died down, all I could hear was the blood pounding inside my head. There are no animals, no birds, no mountains – just an enormous white sheet of ice.

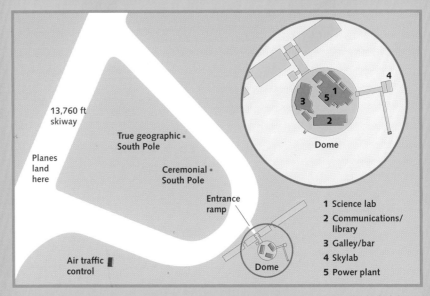

13,760 ft skiway

Planes land here

True geographic South Pole

Ceremonial South Pole

Air traffic control

Entrance ramp

Dome

Dome

1 Science lab
2 Communications/ library
3 Galley/bar
4 Skylab
5 Power plant

This is a plan of Amundsen-Scott South Pole station. See the place marked Skylab? It is a special observation tower.

Wintering at the Pole

For half the year, the South Pole is in complete darkness. About twenty-eight workers remain on station during this period, cut off from the outside world. Each year on 21 June, they celebrate Midwinter's Day. Temperatures can fall as low as -128°F.

Still at the South Pole
Sunday 25 December –
Christmas Day

LONDON, ENGLAND
9759 MILES

This signpost reminds me that I'm a long way from home.

Dear Daniel,

Happy Christmas! Yesterday, on Christmas Eve, we held a candlelit carol service in the dining room. Someone played a guitar to keep us vaguely in tune. Today we have just had a big lunch consisting of tinned vegetables, tinned potatoes and several turkeys, followed by Christmas pudding. It seems funny to be having Christmas dinner when there aren't any Christmas cards up – but at least we have plenty of snow to make up for it.

I am feeling a bit lonely, and I thought of you all sitting round the table at home. I suppose that by the time you read this, Christmas will seem like a long time ago.

Love, Sara

A scientist taking a very short trip around the world...

The race around the world

The most important Christmas tradition at the South Pole is the Race Around the World. It is a 1.9 mile race of 3 circuits around the Pole itself. Competitors travel the course however they like – on skis, skidoos, sledges or even on the back of a caterpillar truck. I took part in this race on foot and came fifty-second.

Meeting the Emperor

I am here

Here I am discussing important matters with the locals.

Halley Station
Thursday 29 December

Dear Daniel,

Guess what happened to us today? We were visited by 10 emperor penguins! Emperors are the largest of all penguins, and they have magnificent mandarin orange streaks on their lower beaks and an orange collar around their necks. They came right up to us, trying to see what we were doing. On land penguins have no predators, which means that they aren't at all scared of people. They were quite chatty - cawing away to each other, and to me. After a while they waddled back towards the sea - I expect it was teatime.

Love, Sara

The emperors of Antarctica.

One thing I noticed straight away about these penguins was their feet. They were scaly and horny and looked very, very ancient. Emperor penguins and king penguins only lay one egg. The father holds the egg on his feet and keeps it warm until it hatches. Then the parents take it in turns to catch fish for the chick to eat. The young first visit the sea when they are about five months old.

The females each lay an egg in May or June, which is the dead of winter down here, and the fathers then look after the eggs for two months of complete darkness. During this time they don't eat or drink, and they huddle together in a large group to keep warm. They take it in turns to stand on the outside, where it's windiest. By the time the sun rises again the male emperors are very thin.

Emperor penguins enjoying an evening stroll.

Emperors are very fast swimmers, and they dive as deep as 848 feet to hunt for fish and squid.

Adélie penguins

There are seven different types of penguin living in and around the Antarctic – rockhoppers, macaroni, king, gentoo, chinstrap, emperor and Adélie. The most common are the Adélies, who live in colonies of as many as 40,000 breeding pairs.

Adélie penguins in their rookery.

The emperor penguins that came up to my tent were about a metre tall. That makes them as tall as a four-year-old human. I thought this was pretty big until one of the scientists in the camp told me that there are fossils of penguins six and a half feet tall! Can you imagine a penguin taller than your dad?

3.2 feet

1.6 feet

William, who is four years old Emperor penguin Gentoo penguin Rockhopper penguin

Seals

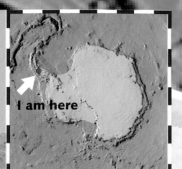

I am here

A. Weddell seal takes it easy.

The Antarctic Peninsula
Tuesday 3 January

Dear Daniel,

I have discovered some seal pups which were born very near our camp. They are Weddells, named after the English sailor James Weddell. This kind lives further south than any other seal as their sharp teeth can keep a hole in the ice open. They smell a bit, and I noticed that their fur was peeling off like wallpaper. At night they bellowed quite loud. Adult Weddells can weigh as much as 1,000 pounds – more than five times as heavy as your dad! Their favorite food is a kind of cod that lives in Antarctic waters, and they also enjoy squid and crustaceans.

Love from Sara

What happens when penguins meet polar bears ?

They never do! Polar bears live up in the Arctic. The North Pole itself is simply floating ice, whereas Antarctica is land. The two polar environments are quite different. Inside the Arctic Circle fresh water flows and plants grow, so animals can live there, whereas only marine creatures like penguins and seals can live in Antarctica. They live off the sea, not the land.

Seals and their pups

Weddells pup (give birth) in September. The babies weigh about 60 pounds when they are born, and because their mothers' milk has a very high fat content they gain as much as 4 pounds in weight a day. I went back to see the pups near our camp every day and they looked as if they were being inflated like balloons.

Newly born pup with its mother.

Divers with crabeater seals.

Diving with seals

Scientists are very interested in how seals function underwater, as they know a seal's heartbeat slows right down to enable it to save oxygen. I met a scientist who goes scuba diving with crabeater seals and keeps a careful record of their behavior. There are more crabeaters than any other kind of seal, and they don't eat crabs! They eat mostly krill, a kind of small prawn.

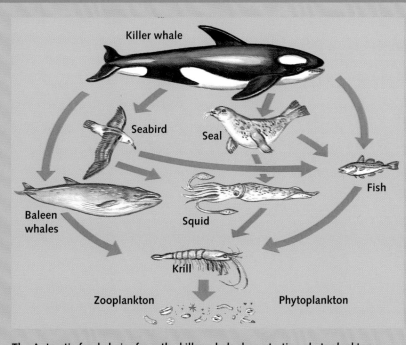

Killer whale

Seabird

Seal

Baleen whales

Squid

Fish

Krill

Zooplankton

Phytoplankton

The Antarctic food chain, from the killer whale down to tiny phytoplankton.

The food chain

The Southern Ocean around Antarctica is teeming with life. At the top of the food chain are whales, who either feed by biting with teeth like we do or through a series of filter plates. Toothed whales enjoy a good dinner of penguin, seal, seabird or fish. The phytoplankton at the very bottom of the food chain get their food from the sun's light.

All Kinds of Ice

I am here

Icebergs

Antarctica is covered by a thick layer of ice like the sugary white icing on a wedding cake. As it builds up, this layer slowly moves out from the center of the continent and eventually reaches the sea, where chunks snap off to form icebergs.

Iceberg floating at sea

Only the tip of an iceberg is visible. Since so much is hidden underwater they can be a danger to ships.

Icebergs form during the summer, when the air temperature is warmer.

The largest iceberg on record is 11,969 square miles – the same size as Belgium.

An iceberg trapped in frozen sea.

Glaciers

Glaciers are formed by huge, close-packed layers of ice moving towards the sea. They often have sheer sides, like cliff faces, and can be as tall as a small mountain. Antarctic glaciers are 'continental', because they spread out from a central mass. The glaciers in Europe are 'alpine', which means they slide down from a high valley.

The Barne glacier on Ross Island. Can you see me standing in front of it?

Ice crystal flowers forming on frozen sea.

A fantastic natural ice sculpture on Mount Erebus.

Fossil Bluff
Sunday 8 January

Dear Daniel,

I have never seen so much ice, and so many different kinds of it too. Antarctica has 90 per cent of the whole world's ice, and in some places it is 4,800 feet deep. Around the edge of the continent even the sea is frozen sometimes, and I often pitch my own tent on it. You have to drill a long way to get through this lid of ice over the sea, but when you do, there are fish living in the chilly waters underneath. They have special anti-freeze in their blood to stop them from icing up.

I am sending you photographs of some of the different kinds of ice I have seen.

Love, Sara

A timeless land

Because the temperature in Antarctica is so low, and because there is such a huge quantity of ice, bacteria cannot live. This means that nothing can go mouldy, like a sandwich does if you leave it in your lunch box for too long, and nothing rots. If seals die on the ice their bodies mummify (dry up). The photograph on the left shows a Weddell seal that has been dead for a hundred years, and although the wind has worn away its fur, its body has been preserved by the cold. Basically, Antarctica functions like a big deep freeze.

Science

I am here

Joce at base camp, preparing her equipment.

McMurdo Sound
Friday 13 January

Dear Daniel,

I've been spending some time with three American scientists, Joce, Lydia and Susan. Joce is a fish biologist, and she has to go fishing to pull up slippery Antarctic cod from the bottom of the Southern Ocean. Lydia collects ice samples and takes them back to her laboratory in California to find out what the atmosphere was like thousands of years ago. (She can do this by examining the bubbles of gas trapped within the ice.) And Susan is a diver. She goes down into the water herself to collect the tiny creatures which live there. I've decided I'd like to be a scientist.

Love, Sara

Collecting ice samples

Lydia drills holes in the ice and pulls out samples. She can take shallow samples by using a hand drill, but deep cores require a team of people, a lot of equipment and days of hard work. This kind of research also happens in the Arctic.

A team of scientists boring deep holes in the ice in order to retrieve long cores. These samples have to be sent home in a deep freeze.

Lydia uses a hand drill to bore a hole in the ice. The drill twists around like a corkscrew.

Diving under the ice

Scuba diving is very different in Antarctica. To start with, you have to make a hole to get under the ice – then find the hole afterwards to get out again. Secondly, the water temperature is 29°F, which means that you have to wear a lot of insulation.

A diver lowers herself through a hole in the ice with the help of her colleagues. The tank on her back contains oxygen.

Wearing lots of layers restricts movement, especially the hands. When divers come out of the water after a dive, the area around their mouths is numb with cold – they talk as if they have just been to the dentist.

Once they are down, the water is so clear they can see as far as 640 feet ahead. Susan told me that when she is diving in Antarctica she feels as if she has entered a secret underwater garden – one that nobody has seen before.

In this cross section you can see how a diver enters the Southern Ocean through a hole in the frozen surface. Deep down divers need light to see the way.

A diver illuminating her way through the depths of the Southern Ocean.

Going fishing

The fish biologist on the right has begun by drilling a small hole, and he is dangling an instrument into it to test the water underneath. The hole will have to be made much larger if fish are to be pulled through.

Biologists themselves sometimes dive down to study Antarctic fish.

And More Science

I am here

I am here

On the left Julia is about to release a balloon. In her right hand you can see the box containing recording equipment. It will dangle from the balloon.

Preparing a balloon before inflating it with helium.

Sending up balloons

Atmospheric scientists in Antarctica are trying to find out what the air is like far above our heads. One of the ways they can measure floating gases is by sending up large balloons carrying small but powerful electronic monitoring equipment. Preparing the balloons involves careful checking of the balloon skin for holes or creases which could tear when it is eventually inflated. When the balloons are up, they send messages back to computers on earth.

The ozone layer

A few years ago a team of British scientists noticed that the layer of ozone over Antarctica had thinned, and that in one place there was even a hole. Ozone is a colorless gas which lies in a kind of blanket around the earth, and, like a blanket, it provides protection. A hole could have very serious consequences, as it leaves the planet exposed.

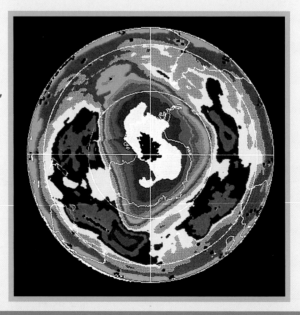

The colors on this satellite picture of the area above Antarctica show the different depths of the ozone layer. The purple color around Antarctica shows where the layer is thinnest.

South Pole and
Victoria Land
Monday 16 January

Dear Daniel,

Because the earth's atmosphere is very shallow over the polar regions, scientists in Antarctica have an excellent 'window' on to the skies. Some of them use telescopes – but they aren't the long thin kind you have seen at home. One of the telescopes I saw at the Pole weighs six tons! It detects short wavelengths in distant galaxies. The scientists who do this kind of work are astrophysicists.

Imagine how difficult it is to get such big equipment down here. It has to be built back at home, taken to pieces, flown to Antarctica then reassembled on the ice. Perhaps I don't want to be a scientist after all. Do you think you would?

Love, Sara

Satellite equipment on Black Island.
It allows the people at McMurdo base
to communicate with the outside world.

Satellites

Satellites orbiting the earth are used to
transmit and receive information
to and from Antarctica. The messages
are picked up by aerials planted firmly
in the ice. On the right you can see
Italian scientists working on an aerial
on the polar plateau. They have to
go back to it at least once a year
to check that it is working properly.

This drawing shows how radio signals are
transmitted to Antarctica via a space satellite.

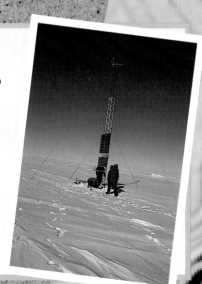

The Race to the Pole

I am here

Cape Evans
Saturday 21 January

Dear Daniel,

I spent the whole morning inside Captain Scott's hut. It was built in 1911 when an expedition arrived by ship from Britain to explore Antarctica, and it has been frozen in time. There are still bottles of Heinz tomato ketchup in the kitchen, and someone's sock rolled up in a ball on the floor. The early explorers didn't have any of the modern conveniences we have. It took them almost a year to get here - and they were away from home for three years at a time. Sometimes they didn't wash for months because it was too cold to undress and anyway, they didn't have any clean clothes.

See you soon.

Love from Sara

Inside Captain Scott's hut.

Captain Scott's hut at Cape Evans on Ross Island.

Roald Amundsen (1872–1928), a Norwegian, was the first man to reach the South Pole. He was already famous as an explorer in northern polar regions.

Ernest Shackleton (1874–1922), an Anglo-Irishman from the merchant navy, was one of the greatest Antarctic explorers ever to have lived. His men were very loyal towards him.

Robert Falcon Scott (1868–1912), the first Englishman to reach the South Pole, was a captain in the Royal Navy. He died while skiing back from the Pole and his body is still buried in the ice.

A desperate struggle

Amundsen and Scott were both trying to reach the South Pole first. The two parties set out from different places and skied all the way to the Pole. Scott and his four companions pulled their own sledges, while Amundsen and his men used husky dogs. The Norwegians beat the British to it by five weeks, and left their flag planted at the Pole.

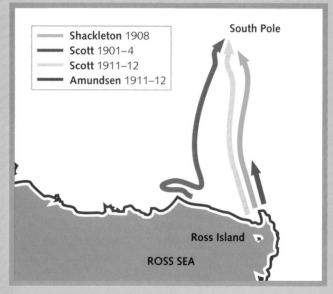

▬▬	**Shackleton** 1908
▬▬	**Scott** 1901–4
▬▬	**Scott** 1911–12
▬▬	**Amundsen** 1911–12

South Pole

Ross Island

ROSS SEA

Routes taken to the Pole. In 1908 Shackleton and his companions got to within 112 miles of the Pole, then turned back due to sickness and bad weather.

Stores outside Shackleton's hut. They've been there for 90 years.

This salt left by Shackleton could be used on your fries.

Historical Antartica

I am here

Fossil Bluff
Thursday 26 January

Dear Daniel,

Ever since Amundsen and Scott's day, people from many countries have been coming to Antarctica on expeditions. Most of them try to ski right across the continent pulling all their equipment – some for over 3,728 miles!

The first woman to set foot on the continent came in 1935. In 1992-3 an American all-women expedition skied to the South Pole, and recently a Norwegian called Liv Arnesen did the same journey alone. It took her 50 days, and she just pitched her tent on the ice sheet every night. At the beginning her sledge weighed 220 pounds – more than your bath filled with sand.

Love from Sara

Members of a Norwegian expedition gather around the South Pole after completing their journey.

Key dates in Antarctic history

1773 James Cook crosses Antarctic Circle and (1775) makes first landing on South Georgia in the Falklands.

1820 Fabien Bellingshausen, an Estonian, makes first sighting of Antarctic continent (probably).

1821 British sealer John Davis becomes the first man to set foot on the Antarctic continent.

1841 English explorer James Clark Ross penetrates pack ice to 78° south.

1898 Belgian expedition becomes the first to winter in the pack ice.

1899 Carsten Borchgrevinck's British expedition winters on the continent.

1901–04 Scott's *Discovery* expedition. Men sledge to 82° south.

1907–09 Shackleton's *Nimrod* expedition. A party sledges to within 97 nautical miles (112 miles) of the Pole.

1910–12 Roald Amundsen's expedition in the *Fram*. A team reaches the South Pole on 15 December 1911.

1910–1913 Scott's *Terra Nova* expedition. Five men reach the South Pole five weeks after Amundsen, and all die on return journey.

1911–14 Douglas Mawson's Australasian Antarctic Expedition to Adélie Land.

1914–17 Shackleton's transantarctic expedition and his epic journey to South Georgia after the ship *Endurance* is wrecked.

1922 Shackleton dies at South Georgia during his third expedition.

1934–37 British Graham Land Expedition discovers that the Antarctic Peninsula is not an archipelago (group of islands).

1935 Caroline Mikkelson becomes the first woman to set foot on the continent.

1947 American Richard Byrd makes a flight over the South Pole.

1955–58 Continent crossed for the first time by explorers Vivien Fuchs and Edmund Hillary's Commonwealth Transantarctic Expedition.

1956 American George Dufek's plane lands at the Pole – the first man there since Scott.

1957–58 International Geophysical Year. Twelve countries establish 60 bases on Antarctica and surrounding islands.

A Chilean research base.

1959 Antarctic Treaty, which applies to all territory south of latitude 60° south, signed by 12 nations.

1961 Antarctic Treaty comes into force.

1991 International agreement on Environmental Protection places a 50-year ban on digging for oil and minerals.

Members of a triumphant Japanese overland expedition arrive at the Pole.

Fun and Games

I am here

Linda has come down the slope the easy way – in a tyre.

Rothera Station
Wednesday 1 February

Dear Daniel,

There's no television here, and so when we have free time we have to make our own entertainment. If the weather is clear we go skiing – either alpine skiing, which means downhill, or cross-country skiing, which is on flat ice. For downhill skiing we take it in turns to tow the skiers uphill behind a skidoo. Some camps have enormous tires which you can sit in and whiz downhill that way. It's called tubing. We sometimes throw parties in the evenings, too, especially if it's someone's birthday.

I shall have to wait for all my birthday presents this year.

Love from Sara

Al, the Rothera Station cook, made me this birthday cake.

Preparing for a Thanksgiving dinner at an American field camp.

Bagpipes and pirates

We have a lot of fun with the pilots from the US Navy who fly American scientists around down here. They call themselves the Ice Pirates. One team of scientists put the sign below on their hut.

How on earth did the New Zealanders get this parking meter down here?

Ian welcomed in the New Year by playing his bagpipes on the balcony of our hut.

Ice art

Last week we had an ice sculpture competition. We cut blocks from the ice using special ice saws then moulded them into shapes. The winning entry was a dragon – it took two mechanics all day to make it. It still shows no sign of melting.

Making the dragon ice sculpture.

Rachel enjoying the sun during a day's skiing.

Vasco skiing, towed behind a snowmobile.

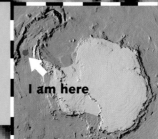

I am here

My last day on the ice.

Afloat in the Southern Ocean
Thursday 9 February

Dear Daniel,

Summer has almost ended and so has my Antarctic journey. I was picked up from Rothera Station, along with ten scientists, by an ice-strengthened ship called the Bransfield. At the moment we are sailing up the Antarctic Peninsula in the direction of the Falkland Islands. The journey will take about ten days, and from there I fly back to England in an RAF (Royal Air Force) plane.

As we left Rothera base the twelve people who are spending the winter there set off flares on the jetty. I feel very sad to be leaving Antarctica – will I ever see another iceberg again?

See you SOON!

Love, Sara

John taking a rest at Rothera Station after unloading from the Bransfield – the ship that took me home.

Winter approaches

As summer draws to a close in Antarctica the sun falls lower and lower in the sky until it eventually sets – and it will not reappear until the winter is over. The Adélie penguins have all migrated north and the sea is beginning to freeze over. It is as if the whole continent is shutting down.

The diagram below shows the earth tilting on its axis. Because of this tilt, Antarctic winters are totally dark whereas in summer it is light all the time.

By February, darkness is beginning to creep over the peninsula.

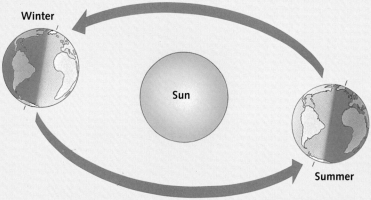

Winter

Sun

Summer

In the depth of winter the South Pole is tilted away from the sun.

In the summer the South Pole is tilted towards the sun.

This pack ice in the Southern Ocean will soon be frozen.

The Falklands

The Falklands archipelago is about half the size of Wales (4,633 square miles) and consists of about 200 islands. Its nearest neighbour is Argentina 398 miles away. The total population is about 2,000.

The view from the ship as we approached Port Stanley, the capital (and only town) of the Falklands.

ATLANTIC OCEAN

Falkland Islands

South America

Rothera Station

This map shows the route the *Bransfield* took after it picked us up from Rothera.

More than half the people on the Falklands live in Stanley. This hotel is off the main street.

Further Reading

Books for Young Readers

Andrist, Ralph K.
HEROES OF POLAR
EXPLORATION
"A Horizon Caravel Book"
New York: American Heritage
Publishing Co., 1962

Baines, John D.
ANTARCTICA
Chatham, NJ: Raintree
Steck-Vaughn, 1997

Green, Jen
EXPLORING THE POLAR
REGIONS
"Voyages of Discovery"
New York: Peter Bedrick Books,
1997

McCurdy, Michael
TRAPPED BY THE ICE!
Shackleton's Amazing Antarctic
Adventure
New York: Walker & Co., 1997

Pringle, Laurence
ANTARCTICA
New York: S&S Children's, 1992

Sauvain, Philip
ROBERT SCOTT IN THE
ANTARCTIC
Parsippany, NJ: Silver Burdett
Press, 1993

Taylor, Barbara
ARCTIC & ANTARCTIC
"Eyewitness Books"
New York: Knopf, 1995

Books for Adults

Fothergill, Alastair
A NATURAL HISTORY OF THE
ANTARCTIC
Orig. title: LIFE IN THE FREEZER
New York: Sterling, 1995

Kirwan, Laurence P.
A HISTORY OF POLAR
EXPLORATION
New York: W.W.Norton, 1960

Lansing, Alfred
ENDURANCE: Shackleton's
Incredible Voyage
New York: McGraw-Hill, 1959
New York: Carroll & Graf, 1986

Shackleton, Ernest
SOUTH
New York: Carroll & Graf, 1998

Wheeler, Sara
TERRA INCOGNITA: Travels in
Antarctica
New York: Random House, 1998

INDEX

A
altitude 23
Amundsen, Roald 13, 37, 39
Antarctic Treaty 9, 39
Arctic 28
Arnesen, Liv 38
atmosphere 23, 34, 35
axis of earth 23, 43

B
bacteria 31
balloons, monitoring 34
bases (stations) 14, 15, 24
Bellingshausen, Fabien 39
boats 20
boots 12
Borchgrevinck, Carsten 39
Byrd, Richard 39

C
camping 16, 18
caterpillar tracks 11
clothes 12, 13
Cook, James 39
cooking 18, 19

D
Davis, John 39
drilling 16, 32, 33, 39
Dufek, George 39

E
environmental protection 39
Evans, Captain 13
explorers 36- 39
eye protection 13

F
Falklands 39, 43
fishing 33
flying 10, 11, 19, 20, 21, 39
food 18, 19, 25
food chain 29
frostbite 14

Fuchs, Vivien 39

G
geodesic dome 24
germs 14, 31
glaciers 9, 17, 30
grounding line 17

H
helicopters 20, 21
Hercules planes 10
Hillary, Edmund 39
hydroponics 15

I
ice crystals 31
ice pick 19
ice sculptures 31, 41
icebergs 30
identification tags 12
igloos 17
inflatable boats 20
insulation 12, 13, 33
international co-operation 9
International Geophysical Year 39

L
latitude lines 8

M
Mawson, Douglas 39
McMurdo Base 14, 15
Mikkelson, Caroline 39
Mount Erebus 11
mummification 31

N
nansen sledges 20, 21

O
ozone layer 34

P
penguins 26, 27
phytoplankton 29
pilots 41

plants in water 15
polar bears 28

R
Race Around the Pole 25
remote controlled vehicles 16, 17
reverse osmosis 14
Ross, James Clark 11, 39
Ross Island 8, 11, 15, 30, 36

S
satellites 35
scientists 17, 32, 33, 34, 35
Scott, Robert Falcon 36, 37, 39
scuba diving 29, 33
seals 28-29, 31
seawater 14
Shackleton, Ernest 37, 39
skidoos 20, 21
skis 11, 40, 41
sledges 19, 20, 21, 37
snow-blindness 13
South Pole 8, 22, 23, 25, 37
Southern Ocean 8, 29, 43
stations (bases) 14, 15, 24
summer 9
Sun 23, 43
supplies 19, 21

T
telescopes 35
temperatures 9, 24
thermal clothes 12
transport 10, 11, 20, 21, 42
Twin Otter planes 11, 19, 20

V
volcanoes 11

W
water 14, 15, 19
Weddell, James 28
whales 29
winter 9, 24, 43

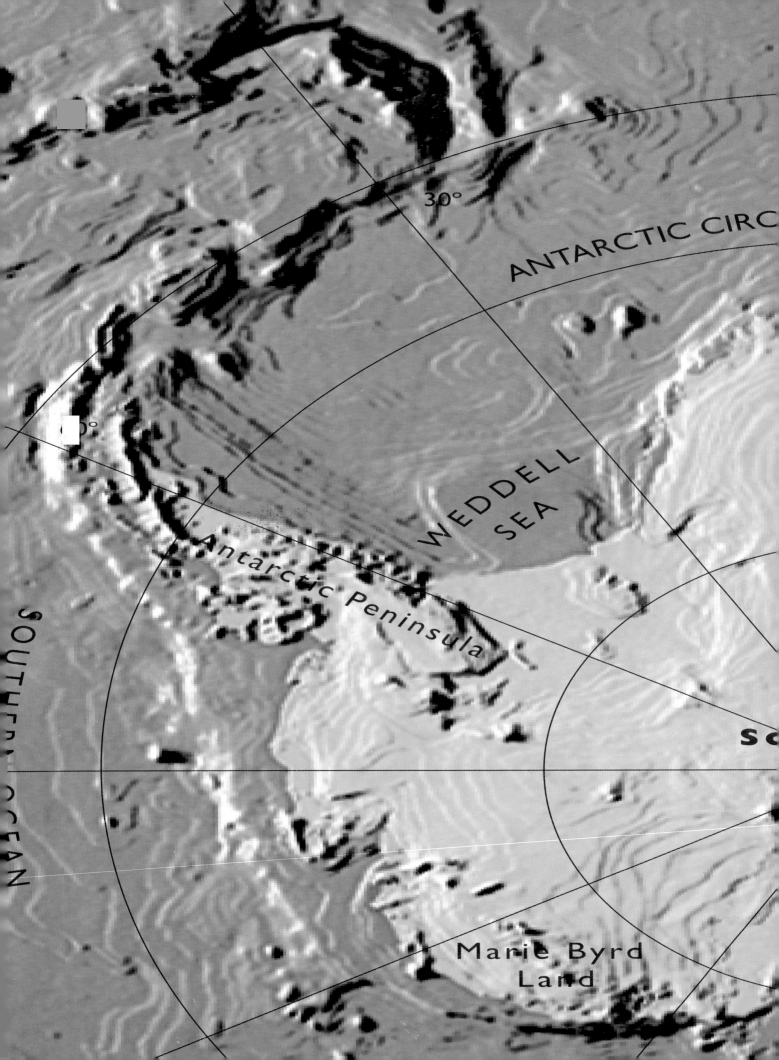